THE LEGACY OF
LEONIDAS I

T.D. VAN BASTEN

TABLE OF CONTENTS

Introduction.. 1

I: Land of the Virtuous... 5

Sparta's Origins.. 10

Mycenaean Origins 11

The Foundation of Sparta 15

The Lycurgus Constitution 18

A Growing Sparta... 21

The Spartan Education... 24

A Semi-Eugenic Society.. 26

Cohesion, Obedience, and Stability 27

A Military City-State 29

Mothers of Men 31

Shocking Virtues.. 33

II: A Man of Sparta..35

Highborn Not Intended to Become King.............. 37

Destined to Be A Hero 40

III: The Battle of Thermopylae 43

The Support of the Greeks....................................... 48

The Power of the Phalanx 49

The Defeat 52

IV: Leonidas' Legacy **55**

Immediate Legacy 58

Legendary Legacy 61

Conclusion **63**

A Note from T.D. van Basten **67**

About the Author **69**

Ancient Greece Biographies **71**

INTRODUCTION

Leonidas is one of the most well-known and remembered of all Sparta's mighty military leaders. The leader of the famous Battle of 300, it was his bravery and cunning that would ultimately propel the Greeks to victory over the invading Persians. He would go down in history as a legendary leader and brave, valiant warrior for his strength in the face of opposition and his selfless willingness to lay down his life for his country.

His rise to kingship was rather unorthodox, but he would go down as one of the most legendary. He showed a keen understanding of how to make the best of the tools one has at their disposal, and to use one's strategy, even in the face of insurmountable odds. He understood that much more than his own fate, that was at stake in the battles he would face. This courage was not only what led to his legendary status, it ultimately gave the Greeks the courage they needed to fend off foreign invaders and remain a sovereign collection of city-states.

He had not been raised to become king, but circumstances would dictate that this be the case. He had, as all other Spartan boys, been trained at the Agoge and was prepared for life as a soldier, not a leader. However, his military prowess would turn out to be a huge advantage for him. He had two older brothers, both of which were in line for the throne before him, but fate would lead him to the kingship, as both brothers died before their father, leaving Leonidas the only heir to the throne.

When the Persians, under Xerxes, decided to invade the Greek mainland, the various city-states joined together in a tentative alliance to help expel the invading forces. Legend has it that before heading off to battle, Leonidas sought the counsel of the Oracle at Delphi who prophesied that a Grecian king must die in battle for Greece to maintain its sovereignty. He took the prophecy to mean that he himself had to be the one to sacrifice his life for the good of the empire and he was willing to make that sacrifice for the future of Greece.

His efforts culminated in the famous Battle of Thermopylae, where for three days, his small band of forces was able to fend off the huge Persian army. It was ultimately a betrayal that gave Persia the upper hand in the conflict. A Grecian shepherd informed Xerxes and his forces of a shortcut whereby they could skirt around the main band of Grecian troops, allowing them to attack the Greeks from both sides.

Leonidas, noticed that this was likely an unwinnable battle, directed most of the troops to retreat. He and his band of 300 hoplites were all that stood in the way of Xerxes. After a hard fought battle, Leonidas was killed in this last stand, along

[2]

with every single one of the 300 remaining men. His death would propel him to legendary status as a warrior and would also give the Greeks the confidence they needed to stay firm and eventually win the war against Persia. Though it would be a year after his fateful death, the Greeks would prevail against the Persians, driving them out permanently and maintaining their sovereignty.

The brave, self-sacrificing efforts of Leonidas and his men would go down in history and lore. Throughout history, he has been propped up as the ultimate warrior, who fought with skill and cunning, and was willing to give up his life for the greater good of the country. He was able to inspire the same feelings of kinship and bravery in his fellow soldiers, which was a key part of their success as warriors. Since he was raised in the brotherhood of warriors, he was able to speak the language of the warrior, making him a huge benefit as king and leader during a tumultuous time in Spartan history.

THE LEGACY OF LEONIDAS I

I

LAND OF THE VIRTUOUS

"Everything has its beauty but not everyone sees it."
—CONFUCIUS

Sparta refers to the Grecian city-state, initially called Lacedaemon, which was located along the Eurotas River. In time, Sparta would become one of the most dominant military land powers in the entirety of the Greek Empire, and perhaps even the world at the time. Though a distinct city-state, Sparta would come to represent the power and might of the Grecian world. The way in which young men were trained to be faithful warriors, from such a young age, would, for many thousands of year, be looked upon as the epitome of the warrior class.

The dominant militarily culture was immense. When wars were fought involving the whole of the Greek empire, such as during the Greco-Roman wars, Sparta stepped up as the leader of military forces and strategy. The citizens of Sparta were pretty much born to be warriors and the focus of their entire life was to provide brave military service to one's city-state. Since they were trained as warriors in the Agoge from such a young age, their skill and dedication was unparalleled, which made them natural leaders for any sort of united military endeavor.

While they were part of the same loosely grouped city-states, infighting would ultimately lead to internal battles within the Greek empire, particularly between Athens and Sparta. One such conflict was the Peloponnesian War, which, while won by Sparta, did not come without great loss of life and pride. These conflicts would continue during the duration of the Grecian Empire as we know it, though conflicts were laid aside at times when outside forces necessitated the city-states work together to defend their lands and honor.

From the inception of Sparta as a distinct city-state, war was in the blood of the people. The original constitution of the country, which was admired around the ancient world, was dedicated to producing a cohesive and stable social structure that would blindly adhere to the laws of the land and willingly put one's body on the line should the need arise. The training of men as warriors was a key part of society and was seen as the virtuous way of life for a decent Spartan. Due to the regular conflict the Spartans engaged in, this would suit them very well throughout their rise to the top of the Grecian Empire.

Sparta, it should be noted, was an incredibly stratified society. In short, there was a huge difference between the so-called "haves" and the "have nots." It was akin to a caste system in that there was no way to move beyond your social strata and it was one you were born into. There was great inequality between the different subgroups within the population. It could be said that Sparta was split up into a quasi-caste system that was comprised of Spartiates, which were full Spartan citizens, Mothakes, which were non-Spartan free men, Perioikoi, which were freed men, and Helots, which were state-owned serfs/slaves and non-Spartan locals.

The Spartiates were the future military class of Spartan society. From an early age, they were sent for extensive military training at the highly specialized training facility referred to as the Agoge. Here, they would learn physical fitness, military strategy, and much more that would help prepare them in their future as warriors and contributing citizens.

Women, while still quite repressed by our standards, enjoyed many more freedoms in Sparta than they did elsewhere. In Sparta, women were the dominant decision makers of the domestic household. They were allowed to own and inherit property, as well as to dispose of their wealth as they saw fit. Young girls were even required to participate in sport in a competitive arena, just as the boys were. For these reasons, women in Sparta were certainly the most free amongst the city-states, if not the world at the time. It would be hard for one to claim that women in Sparta were treated fairly, but the rights they enjoyed were revolutionary for the time and women did not regain many of these rights for some thousands of years. It is due to the need for men to be free for military service that necessitated women taking a more active role in the home and their own lives, but this necessity allowed them a degree of freedom and self-determination that women in other parts of Greece and the rest of the world could only dream of.

1

From an early age, the Spartiates were sent for extensive military training at the highly specialized training facility referred to as the Agoge.

Sparta's Origins

Much of what we know about the origins of Sparta is steeped in legend, which obfuscates fact from fiction, so chances are, the actual details are forever lost to the proverbial sands of time. Most point to Mycenaean and Dorian roots for the society. The Mycenaeans were the earliest inhabitants of the region during the Grecian era. They lived along Eurotas region until what became known as the "Dorian Invasion." We know a little about the life and times of these predecessors, but many details of the great story have been lost, thus leaving us with a murky picture of the actual evolution of the society.

After the invasion, the Dorians would alter the culture of the region and become the dominant culture. It was these people who would directly give rise to the city-state of Sparta. Due to the lack of archaeological record, as well as written history, much of what we know about the development of the Spartan state is found in legend and speculation. We will likely never know the true turn of events that led to the rise of what we now know of as Sparta.

MYCENAEAN ORIGINS

The Mycenaeans lived in settlements along the banks of the Eurotas River from roughly 1600-1100 BC. The peak of the Mycenaean civilization was around 1350 BC when the settlement boasted a major citadel, as well as a population of some 30,000 people. The earliest known literary reference to this region came from the writings of Homer. Much of what we know about this early precursor to Sparta is steeped in legend, so where fact and fiction actually diverge is not entirely known.

Early legend states that Mycenae was founded by Perseus, who was the son of Danae and Zeus. After having accidentally killed his grandfather, Acrisius of Argos, Perseus became unable to inherit the land and position that were intended for him. To remedy this problem, Perseus simply traded kingdoms with his cousin. His cousin would come to rule Argos, while Perseus became the king of the Tiryns and founded Mycenae. Whether or not these were actual people or events, again, is lost to time, but these legends would prove to be very important to the Spartan people's image of themselves and their heritage.

Perseus went on to marry Andromeda and father many children. However, interestingly enough, he would later die in a battle against his cousin's forces in Argos. His unexpected death led to chaos about the appropriate line of succession to the throne. When a king dies an untimely death without adequately articulating who the heir to the throne is, confusion and conflict will almost likely occur. This is something that has been seen time and time again in the history of countries where kingship is inherited or passed on by the former ruler.

By the third ruler of the Perseid dynasty, politically motivated marriages were being employed to help bring about peace and stability to the region. Sthenelus married Nicippe, who was the daughter of King Pelops of Elis, an incredibly powerful and influential region in the area. Their son, Eurystheus, would be the last major ruler of Mycenae in the Perseid dynasty.

Chaos threatened to take hold once again and the people of Mycenae were instructed to choose a Pelopid for their king via an oracle. The field was narrowed down to just two potential rulers. Thyestes was chosen, then, due to circumstances that have not been passed down with the rest of the history, the other candidate, Atreus, was chosen instead.

In an interesting turn of events, Atreus was killed by Thyestes' son, Aegisthus. After the murder, Thyestes was returned to the throne. This would not last long. Atreus' sons, with the help of some powerful forces, were able to drive Thyestes into exile. Tyndareus, the king of Sparta at the time, was one of the powerful allies in the ouster of Thyestes. Once the overthrow had taken places, Tyndareus married his two daughters to Artreus' sons.

Agamemnon married Clytemnestra and went on to rule the land still referred as Mycenae. The other brother, Menelaus, married the daughter Helen and would go on to rule Sparta. As history notes, Helen would end up eloping with Paris of Troy. These events would lead to the famous Trojan War, which ended with a narrow victory by the Greeks. Like much of ancient history, it was assumed that the Trojan War written about by Homer was a mythical epic until the place was actually found some hundred years ago. There is a chance that some of these other seemingly legendary or mythical places and people may be revealed as real in the course of time and discovery.

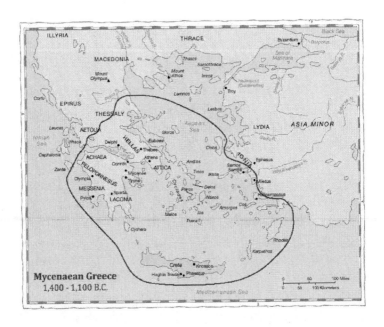

Mycenaean Greece
1,400 - 1,100 B.C.

2.

The Mycenaeans lived in settlements along the banks of the Eurotas River from roughly 1600-1100 BC.

THE FOUNDATION OF SPARTA

There are many legends that surround the rise of the city-state of Sparta. The region that we call Sparta was actually called Lacedaemon, after the mythical king of the region known as Laconia. Lacedaemon was the son of the nymph Taygete and Zeus. He would go on to marry Sparta, who was the daughter of the powerful Eurotas (which the local river would be named for). Lacedaemon named the country after himself and the main settlement after his wife.

Though it is debated as to whether it was an actual event or series of events, many historians have posited a so-called Dorian Invasion to explain the changes in language and culture that occurred during the foundation of Sparta. These changes in language and customs are what really marks the difference between the Greece of antiquity and what we would think of as the Classical Greek society. It may be a bit unwise to refer to it as an invasion, as no historians believe that these changes were the result of a single battle, but rather a gradual change in culture over time. Since we do not know the chain of events that led to this change, it has been seen as convenient for historians to refer to this change as an invasion.

Legend states that the Dorians conquered the region of Lacedaemon/Sparta in what was dubbed the Return of the Heracleidae. The "Return" refers to the conquering and acquisition of the Peloponnesus region. Whether or not this was an actual battle or some other series of events is not known. What we do know is that this event resulted in the reemergence of the descendants of Heracles, who had been previously exiled from the region. Their reemergence as key figures of power and influence in this society is also part of the implications of the "Return."

Hyllus, a Perseid in control of the region at the time, would be killed by Echemus of Arcadia, thus paving the way for the Dorian Invasion. The Dorian people united with the exiled Herakleid forces. This newly formed, single community, then occupied and eventually overtook the lands we now know of as Sparta.

3.

There are many legends that surround the rise of the city-state of Sparta. Though it is debated as to whether it was an actual event or series of events.

THE LYCURGUS CONSTITUTION

The so-called Lycurgus Constitution is also referred to as simply the Spartan Constitution or the Politeia. This would become the rule of law of the land until Sparta became part of the Roman Empire many centuries later. This set of rules helped dictate the law and way of life for all Spartans and many around the ancient world would look upon this constitution with awe and respect.

At this time in the region, the Dorian heritage of the Spartans was incredibly important to the people. It is what defined their language, customs, and regional identity. In Sparta, a different language was spoken than in other city-states in the Greek empire. This gave them a sense of a unique heritage and culture and their rule of law would only add to this notion.

The Constitution was written to help define the Spartan system of social stratification and an almost extreme focus of defense and military prowess. Most of the constitution related to the requirements of Spartan men to be obedient and observe military rule above any other. It was what would ultimately shape their system of education and training that was heavily reliant on regimented military training and state allegiance.

According to myth, Lycurgus, the famous law maker, convened with the god Apollo via the oracle at Delphi to come up with the laws of the land. He received what the Greeks called a "rhetra" or a divine proclamation. Included in this proclamation were instructions as to how to separate society into distinct classes, the creation of a 30 member senate, as well as allowances for assembly and participation. It is thought that, outside the constitution, there were no other recognized laws in Sparta. The constitution was the law. Period. It must be noted that some of the democratic elements Westerners have come to appreciate in our own systems of governance can, in part, be traced back to places of antiquity like Sparta.

The Constitution banned the use of personal currency or coinage. Only official iron obols were to be used and accepted. This meant that personal bartering and individual currency was not accepted or tolerated. Breaking the law in ancient Sparta could have truly dire consequences. To be a good Spartan citizen meant that one stayed fit and was always ready for battle. It meant that one maintained productive farm land for the good of the state, and also had a family. Interestingly, Spartan women were the only Greek women with property rights and the ability to participate in sport. Physical fitness, as a key element of society, was extended to both sexes.

The land was traditionally ruled by two hereditary kings, which was an unusual occurrence that has never been fully explained. Both of the hereditary kings were selected from the powerful bloodline of Heracles.

A Growing Sparta

As the city-state grew in power and size, the organization of the political system had to evolve. In addition to the two hereditary kings, Ephors were elected officials that would serve in the executive branch with the kings. Ephors were quite powerful and influential and were chosen by the citizenship. These elected officials mark one of the first instances of democratic governance. The Ephors were chosen every year and were not allowed to serve more than one term. It were positions like these that many in the Western world would later look to for inspiration when developing their own systems of governance.

The Gerousia was a council of elders, all aged 60 and over, who would serve in this position for life. These elders were often from royal and noble bloodlines. The purpose of the council was to discuss problems and potential policy decisions and then take their findings to the executive branch for a final decision. They also had a role to play when it came to determining the fitness of boys born in Sparta.

The Apella referred to the whole of the eligible voting population in Sparta. While they could not set an agenda, offer policy proposals, or even inquire about details or raise concerns, they were able to vote between the list of options provided to them. When a referendum was issued, the Apella would vote to determine which course of action was taken. This gives them some semblance of control over the governance of their nation.

As noted earlier, the society was broken down into three distinct classes. Spartiates were full citizens and considered part of the Damos. In order to be a Spartiate, one had to be able to trace their lineage back to Sparta's origins, and must have also successfully been trained at the Agoge. At age 20, they received full rights as Spartan citizens until he could no longer contribute his share of grain. They were required to sleep in the barracks until they reached the age of 30, regardless of their marital status. They were also made to dine with the other Spartiates daily until they were no longer worthy of battle, around age 60. Spartiates were not allowed to participate in manufacturing or trade and they were not allowed to travel outside of Sparta unless as a part of a military campaign.

The Perioki were free, but not full, citizens of Sparta. They lived in separate villages and settlements on the edge of town and were allowed a good deal of power for self-governance. They were allowed to own land and were required to supply men for the military, as well as abide by Spartan foreign policy. They were, however, also the ones who were responsible for all the manufacturing and trade for Sparta, and were allowed to travel outside of Sparta for certain reasons.

The Helots were the state-owned serfs or slaves that made up the bulk of the population. Some estimate that as much as 90% of the population was comprised of Helots. These individuals were predominately gleaned from conquered lands such as with the Messenians after the first Messenian War. The Helots would perform a vast bulk of the work that was considered unfit to be performed by those in the other two classes.

THE SPARTAN EDUCATION

All male citizens of Sparta, with the exception of the first born sons in the Eurypontid and Agiad ruling families, were required to undergo rigorous training at the facility referred to as the Agoge. While the focus of the training provided here was mostly military in nature, students also learned stealth and survival tactics, the importance of obedience to authority and honor to country, as well as speaking/communications, dancing, hunting, and, of course, extensive military training.

Agoge means "rearing," but was thought to, in this instance, refer more to the concept of "learning, guidance, and training." Legend states that the mythical Lycurgus founded the Agoge, but there is little to back this up. Most historians believe that the Agoge was founded sometime between the 7-6th centuries BC. This institution would go on to be lauded by many nations in the ancient world and many military educational institutions of today use some of the elements of the Agoge in their training regimen.

Male citizens trained at the Agoge from age 7 to 29, however, one's service to the country and participation in certain regimented elements was not finished when a man reached this age. The aim was to produce solid, capable citizens to fight and serve in the Spartan army. Conformity and what is best for the state was ingrained in them from the start of their education. Lycurgus was said to have ordered the destruction of the walls that protected Sparta, instead claiming that the highly trained men of the Spartan army would become the proverbial wall of Sparta.

Infighting and even theft were encouraged as it was believed that these activities helped hone skills that were highly useful in battle. Stealth, the ability to make a quick decision between life and death, and the assertion of dominance over the group were seen as virtuous.

The Agoge was a prestigious institution that was lauded around the Greek empire. Many powerful families throughout the empire would strive to have their sons accepted to the Agoge, but while a few made the cut, the Spartans were incredibly picky as to who they allowed in.

The training was broken down into three separate parts; paides, which lasted from ages 7-17, paidiskoi, which lasted from ages 17-19, and hebontes, which lasted from ages 20-29.

A SEMI-EUGENIC SOCIETY

Fitness was seen as extremely important to the stability and cohesion of Spartan society. When a baby boy was born, they would be bathed in wine as it was believed that this made the child stronger. The elder council, the Gerousia, then examined the child for fitness, health, and future potential as a warrior.

Not all children were seen as fit to serve. Those who did not make the proverbial grade were slated for death or servitude. The "unfit" child would be left at the base of Mt. Taygetus, where the child would die of exposure, be taken in by a peasant, or in some cases, survive the ordeal. If the child did survive, chances are they would end up in the Helot class of society.

Marriages to foreigners were practically unheard of. The Spartans were proud people who believed in the "purity" of their citizens. The state advised on age of marriage. For women, the ideal age for marriage, as determined by the state, was age 20, much older than in many other city-states. For men, the ideal age for marriage was 30. Marriage to the Spartans was not really seen in the same way as we do today. The purpose was mostly for the creation of future Spartan warriors.

A MILITARY CITY-STATE

Military might, pretty much since the inception of Sparta as a distinct region, was almost the whole of the Spartan identity. The structure and functioning of the society was organized to put an emphasis on qualities that fostered good warriors and obedient citizens.

Military endeavors would be undertaken for any number of reasons. In some cases, it seemed that battle was seen as a way to build national morale. In other cases, battles were waged in order to obtain populations to make up the Helot class of society. In other instances, war was undertaken so as to obtain more land for Spartan citizens. And, of course, there were plain defensive or offensive battles that were sparked by political reasons.

While the Spartan warrior was a fearsome foe that was highly trained, this is not to say that they were without weakness. One of their first tastes of defeat was at the hands of what were referred to as hoplites. Hoplites were citizen soldiers that used spears and shields while in the fearsome phalanx formation. They took the name hoplite from the circular hoplon shield they carried into battle.

Argos, which was a long-time rival of Sparta, was one of the first Greek city-states to introduce the hoplite and phalanx formation in tandem. When the Spartans were faced with this revolutionary fighting force, they were unable to come out of the battle victorious. The Spartans took this loss to heart, but they also took note of the new tactic. They would too begin to employ the use of hoplites in the phalanx position in future battles.

4.

Hoplites were citizen soldiers that used spears and shields while in the fearsome phalanx formation.

MOTHERS OF MEN

Women in Sparta enjoyed freedom and rights that were unheard of anywhere else in the Grecian world. In fact, some of the rights they were granted were unheard of anywhere in the world until just recently. Women in Sparta were often married between the ages of 18-20, which was far older than in the rest of the Greek empire, allowing them time for education and other growth opportunities.

They did not have the right to vote, but it seems that they were educated and even encouraged to discuss "the issues." This led many to believe that, while they were behind the scenes, their opinions were highly influential on their husbands and sons.

Women in Sparta could own property. They were even responsible for almost a third of the land ownership in Sparta. They were allowed to use their wealth as they saw fit. Daughters were also allowed to inherit property or money.

The women in Sparta were said to be outspoken and independent due to the freedom they had in the running of their households. With the males gone much of the time training or at war, the women were responsible for the bulk of the domestic decision making.

[31]

Much to the chagrin of the rest of the region, the women of Sparta were also permitted to dress "scantily" if they chose too. There were no taboos against even married women showing a bit of skin.

Girls were educated as youngsters and were even allowed, if not required, to participate in competitive sports. It has been speculated that the girls may have competed nude before a mixed audience as well. This is something that many today might find shocking, but it was seen as a normal part of Spartan life that instilled in girls the importance of fitness.

Since they only had to raise their sons until the age of 7, there was a lot of spare time to pursue other interests and hobbies, which is not a privilege that many other women at the time neither had nor were allowed. Actually, we don't even happen to see that a lot with current mothers in our modern century.

The case of women in Sparta was extremely rare, even up to this day in certain parts of the world. Mentioned by Plutarch in his "Moralia," Gorgo—the wife of Leonidas—when she was asked "how can *only* the Spartan women rule men?" She answered simply; "because we're also the *only* ones giving birth to men."

SHOCKING VIRTUES

It is easy to look back on ancient cultures as "backwards" or "immoral" but this is actually pretty unfair. While they did run their societies very differently than we do today, the rules they put in place were just as well thought out and debated upon as the mores of today. However, because we come from a different culture with different values and taboos, it can be difficult to accept some of the traits or activities that the Spartans considered virtuous.

As was stated before, due to the importance placed on being the best warrior possible, theft, violence, and even murder were not only permitted, but encouraged. We see this as barbaric, but the Spartans believed it was important to find as many different training and learning opportunities as possible. At the Agoge, boys were often sent out on survival quests where they would be tasked with surviving in the elements and killing any Helots they thought might cause problems or instability in the future. To the Spartans, to be fit and war ready meant that one warrior should be able to dispatch with six Helots.

In Spartan society, the whole was always more important than the individual, so there was no room for personal desires as a member of this society. Fitness was seen as more important than the sanctity of life. They did not see the value in committing effort and resources to those who would be unable to carry their proverbial weight as citizens. This resulted in the accepted practice of infanticide.

Many look at the marital structure and the acceptance of "deviant" sexual behaviors as indicative of a debauched society.

II

A MAN OF SPARTA

"Only the dead have seen the end of the war."
—PLATO

Leonidas I was the son of Anaxandridas II of Sparta. He was the third born son of the king and thus was not in line to become heir to the throne. Leonidas was part of the Agiad dynasty and is alleged to have been descended from the famous warrior Heracles. Though not intended for the throne, circumstances would see Leonidas become King of Sparta.

As the warrior-king of Sparta, Leonidas I would go on to become a famous leader that fought the Persians valiantly in the Second Persian War and the famous battle of 300 at Thermopylae. Much about his life has been lost to history, but we know that he was a well-trained warrior that took his duty seriously. He saw it as his fate and destiny to lead

Greece in battle against the Persians and due to the prophecy of an Oracle, he even knew that his destiny was to pay the ultimate price—his life. To save Greece and Sparta, he was willing to make this sacrifice.

HIGHBORN NOT INTENDED TO BECOME KING

Leonidas I was born the second child of the king's main wife. King Anaxandridas' first wife was long thought to be barren as they had tried for an heir unsuccessfully. The king was encouraged to find a new wife, but for whatever reason, he refused to abandon his first wife. Though Spartans traditionally only took one wife, special privilege was granted to Anaxandridas, allowing him to maintain his primary marriage, while also taking on a second wife for the purposes of fathering an heir to the throne.

Shortly after marrying his second wife, she gave birth to a son, Cleomenes. A year later, his first wife would give birth to a son as well, Dorieus, who was shortly followed by Leonidas, born in an unknown year circa 540 BC.

As the third in line for the throne, there was never any intention of raising Leonidas as an heir. There were two brothers in front of him for the honor. This means that, under Spartan law, he was subject to the same rules and responsibilities as all other citizens of Sparta. This meant that he was to receive the rigorous military training at the Agoge that all other male Spartan citizens were required to undergo.

When he did become king later in life, Leonidas I was one of the rare few kings that had any direct military training or education. It was pretty much unheard of for a king of Sparta to have attended the Agoge as a child.

Leonidas' half-brother, Cleomenes, succeeded Anaxandridas' to the throne upon his death in 520 BC. His half-brother, Dorieus, was furious that Cleomenes was chosen as the heir to the throne when it was Dorieus who was the true first born son of Anaxandridas and his main wife. This anger eventually led him to abandon his homeland of Sparta and attempt to start his own empire in Africa. His efforts were, unfortunately for him, not successful in the slightest.

After his failures in Africa, Dorieus decided to try his luck in Sicily. While he did initially have some success, it was short lived and he would die here not long after arriving.

The details of the relationship between Leonidas I and his brother and half-brother are not well known. We have lost much to the proverbial sands of time. What we do know is that Cleomenes had but one child, a daughter named Gorgo. Leonidas I and Gorgo would be married, but this union took place well before Leonidas took the kingship.

Cleomenes retained the throne as tensions between Greece and Persia reached a tipping point. Persia demanded Grecian submission to Persian authority, something that the Spartans vehemently opposed. Somewhere along the way his half-brother was said to have "lost it" and gone insane. These claims would eventually lead to his exile from Sparta, leaving Leonidas as the unlikely heir to the throne.

Leonidas' relationship with Gorgo appears to have been rather unconventional in that she seemed to have a big influence on his decision making. Evidence shows that her opinion was also highly influential to her father, Cleomenes, as well. This is rather unprecedented as it was uncommon for us to even know the name of a Spartan queen, let alone know anything about any power she might wield.

Gorgo would famously "decipher" a blank tablet that had been sent to the kingship. Thinking that there was more to the blank tablet than met the eye, she hinted that she thought it might be some sort of cipher. When the wax on the tablet was scratched away, it revealed a warning about an impending invasion by Persia. Without her quick thinking, the Spartans would have been caught off guard.

DESTINED TO BE A HERO

Shortly after Leonidas's ascent to the throne, Persia was once again threatening to invade Greece, something that the Spartans fought vehemently to resist. King Xerxes of Persia hoped to subdue Greece in its entirety after his father's failed attempts to take the region.

The Athenians and the Spartans joined together in their efforts to resist the invasion of the Persians. Athenian and Spartan forces were significantly outnumbered as many city-states in the region either remained neutral in the conflict, or submitted to Persian rule.

When Athens requested the assistance of Sparta in resisting the Persian invasion, Leonidas and some key Spartans sought the counsel of the Oracle at Delphi. According to legend, the Oracle gave a stunning prophecy in hexameter verse. The prophecy stated that unless a descendant of Heracles died in battle against the Persians that the city-state of Sparta would fall under control of the Persian army. Basically, a Spartan king had to die in battle in order to save Sparta from being overtaken.

Leonidas took this prophecy incredibly seriously and saw it as his fate to die in battle for his city-state if they had any hope of maintaining their sovereignty. He valiantly accepted his fate and agreed to lead Spartan and Athenian troops in battle. These efforts would culminate in the famous battle of 300 at Thermopylae that would ultimately lead to his death. He would, however, be remembered as one of the bravest warrior-kings in the history of both Sparta and also Greece as a whole.

5.

King Xerxes of Persia attending the lashing and chaining of the Hellespont.

DESTINED TO BE A HERO

III

THE BATTLE OF THERMOPYLAE

"A man's character is his fate."
—HERACLITUS

Thermopylae is a mountainous region near the Aegean Sea in northern Greece. This was the site of the famous "Battle of 300" in 480 BC. Fought between the Greeks and the Persians, this battle saw the Greeks drastically outnumbered. During this siege, Leonidas and his troops managed to hold back the huge Persian army for three trying days, before the Greeks were betrayed by one of their own. The battle, while ultimately unsuccessful, took a huge toll on the Persians under the tutelage of Leonidas.

As had been prophesied by the Oracle at Delphi, Leonidas would die in this heroic siege. His death not only saw the coming to fruition of prophecy, it sealed his name in the category of legends that we still speak of today. Within a year of the famous battle that cost Leonidas his life, the Greeks would finally expel the Persians from the Greek mainland in the battles at Plataea and Salamis.

The context of this conflict went back before the time of Leonidas' rule. Tensions between the Greeks and the Persians had been mounting for some time before the fateful battle of the 300 and Leonidas' death. Under Darius of Persia, attempts—some successful, some unsuccessful—to take the Greek mainland were mounted. The motivation of this conquest is not known as it does not appear to have had anything to do with material resources or land. Some speculate that Darius wanted to subdue the Greeks that had so long resisted his rule.

The threats from the Persians led to a tentative alliance between Sparta and Athens, who had been in a number of skirmishes between themselves. However, when a common enemy from the outside threatened, they were able to bury the proverbial hatchet and join forces. In 490 BC, Persian troops were sent to subdue the Greeks. This effort was met with unexpected force and the Persians were ultimately defeated at the battle at Marathon.

While this may have marked the end for Darius, the tentative truce between Greece and Persia would be short-lived. When Darius died in 486 BC, his son, Xerxes, ascended to the throne. He fully intended to finish what his father had failed to do. As soon as he came to power he began to bulk up the needed infrastructure as well as build up the military.

When the Greeks found out that a massive force of Persians was headed their way, some 10,000 hoplites were deployed to a valley near the base of Mt. Olympos. When it quickly became apparent just how outnumbered they were, the Greeks reluctantly backed off. Though relations between the various city-states, particularly Sparta and Athens, had always been tense, they were willing to join together in an attempt to fend off the Persian invaders.

Some 7,000 troops were soon sent to hold the strategic mountain pass at Thermopylae. The Persians had to get through this pass if they were to enter the Greek mainland where they hoped to conquer the Greeks. These troops came mostly from Athens, Sparta, and Thebes. Many city-states were unwilling to send forces for defense for a number of reasons. Many did not feel it was wise to send so many troops up north, and others, who saw Mt. Olympos as sacred, refused to partake in battle in its shadow. Additionally, many city-states wished to remain neutral in the conflict and some even acquiesced to Xerxes.

Thermopylae was a great place to mount a strategic defense. The Greeks were familiar with the terrain and there was already an ancient fortification wall that they were able to repair. The narrow pass required the massive force of Persian troops to walk in file lines that made them much more manageable to the smaller army. The small band of Greek troops was up against some 80,000 Persian troops.

Before the battle began, there was a 4-day standoff where Xerxes waited for the Greeks to retreat or surrender in the face of such huge forces. On day 4, Xerxes told the Greeks to lay down their arms in order to prevent battle and bloodshed. Leonidas famously replied "molon labe," which can be roughly translated as "come and get it." With that, the battle commenced.

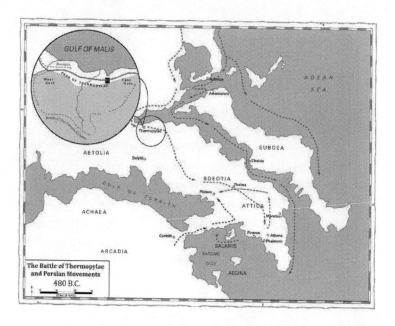

6.

Thermopylae is a mountainous region near the Aegean Sea in northern Greece. This was the site of the famous "Battle of 300" in 480 BC, fought between the Greeks and the Persians.

THE SUPPORT OF THE GREEKS

Tensions between the various city-states had always been a bit tentative and internal warfare had long been a part of the proverbial equation. When a threat from the outside presented itself, the city-states decided to put aside their differences and join forces. As noted earlier, many of the city-states refused to send troops as they wanted to maintain neutrality or give in to Xerxes's demands. This means that a bulk of the troops had to be supplied by Athens and Sparta.

It was quickly decided that Leonidas should lead the troops as he had already shown himself to be an adept and skillful warrior and leader. Having previously sought the counsel of the Oracle at Delphi, who predicted that a Greek king would have to die in battle in order for the Greek empire to maintain its sovereignty, Leonidas assumed this fate to be his. He was willing to lay down his life in battle to ensure the continuity of Greece as a federation of city-states.

THE POWER OF THE PHALANX

When the two forces met for battle, it was essentially a battle between two classical methods of warfare. It would be, in essence, a battle between archers and hoplites, or troops adept at long-range and close-quarters battle respectively. These methods of warfare would be staples of much ancient warfare for centuries to come.

The Persians utilized long-range archers which were followed by a cavalry unit, including the fearsome and highly armed "immortals." The archers had lightweight armor that was not particularly durable, whereas the immortals had better protection and weaponry, making them a formidable foe. For many centuries, this had been the "traditional" form of warfare.

The Greeks utilized hoplites in the phalanx position. The phalanx was a tightly clustered line of soldiers. They were armed with sturdy bronze shields, as well as powerful swords and spears. This type of methodology was better suited to hand-to-hand and close-quarters combat. It was difficult for the long-range forces to penetrate, and due to their heavy shields it was difficult to inflict much damage on soldiers in the phalanx formation.

While the Persians were able to send an impressive volley of arrows at the hoplites, this did little damage to the Greeks who were highly protected by their sturdy shields. Some said that so many arrows were leveled at the Greeks that they had the pleasure of fighting in the shade. The Persian archers, however, had lightweight wicker shields which provided little protection in close-quarters combat situations.

Since the battle took place in a narrow mountain pass, the methods of the Greeks were more effective, though the Persians had them drastically outnumbered. On the first day, Xerxes sent his immortals in an effort to cross the pass, but the small band of Greek soldiers were able to hold strong and resist. The second day of battle ended with much the same result—the Greeks were able to hold firm and retain control of the pass.

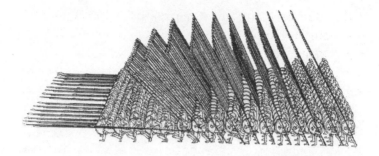

7.

The phalanx was a tightly clustered line of soldiers. They were armed with sturdy bronze shields, as well as powerful swords and spears.

The Defeat

The Greeks, despite being vastly outnumbered, were able to maintain the upper-hand in the first days of the battle, but this success was to be short-lived. Not because of any error on the part of Leonidas or the Greek forces, but because there was a traitor in their ranks. The weakness of one link in the proverbial chain, as we've seen time and time again throughout history, can often be the downfall of many.

Ephialtes, son of Eurydemos, and a local shepherd from the region of Trachis, thought he might gain favor with Xerxes by passing along secret information. He showed the Persians an alternate route that would allow them to skirt around the bulk of the Greek forces unopposed. This allowed the Persians to avoid further casualties and sneak up on the Grecian troops in an ambush style fashion.

Leonidas already had a contingent of Phokian troops there to guard this vital route, but there certainly were not enough forces to expel and defeat the entire Persian military, complete with Immortals. However, when the Persians took them off guard, the Greek troops were forced to retreat to higher ground in an effort to defend against this unexpected onslaught.

The retreat essentially cleared the way for the Persians to cross into the Greek mainland and come in behind the Greek forces. Before their only means of escape was clogged by Persian warriors, Leonidas ordered a large portion of the Greeks to withdraw from the area. It was if he could see what was coming and did not wish for his forces to suffer any more casualties than absolutely necessary. Some may see this as a death wish on the part of Leonidas, but it may also have been what saved the bulk of the Grecian troops to fight another day on another battlefront.

Leonidas, with his remaining small band of forces, comprised of Spartans, Thespians, and Thebans, rallied for a final confrontation with the Persians. They were determined to defend the mountain pass to the last Greek warrior. They hoped that their efforts would stall the Persians and allow time for Greek reinforcements to arrive. That help, sadly, never materialized.

When the hoplites met Xerxes in battle, he was able to launch an attack on both sides of the small band of Greek warriors, essentially boxing them in. Leonidas had his men take up position in the widest part of the pass in an effort to engage his entire force in tandem. It was during this final stand that Leonidas was killed in battle.

The remaining hoplites attempted to seek refuge behind the fortification wall, but the Persian forces were too powerful. Ultimately, they could not mount a successful defense against this terrific onslaught and all of the warriors in this contingent were killed in battle.

With the land forces overrun, the sea forces, which included a number of triremes, were the last line of defense. The Greeks and Persians clashed at sea. The Greeks had a slight advantage as the Persians had been beaten down by poor weather conditions before arriving to battle. Weary Persian naval officers faced a stiff Grecian naval defense. However, when the news of Leonidas's death reached the Greek navy, they withdrew to Salamis, thus ending the Battle of Thermopylae.

IV

LEONIDAS' LEGACY

"The art of living well and the art of dying well are one."
—EPICURUS

Even before his death at the Battle of Thermopylae, Leonidas was a well-respected military leader of Sparta. He had a long history of success in battle and had earned the respect of his men and peers alike. His death at the Battle of Thermopylae was, to many, the fulfillment of the prophecy made by the Oracle at Delphi that stated that a king of Greece would have to lay down his life in order to assure the continuation of the Grecian empire. This fulfillment of prophecy was part of his legend, but also his unwavering strength and courage in the face of insurmountable opposition.

He was given almost legendary and mythical status in Spartan and the greater Greek society pretty much as soon as he died in battle and his legend remains strong to this day. He had a devotion to duty and a sense of history as to the importance of ultimately winning the battle against the Persians, even if he didn't live to see the culmination of his efforts. It should be noted that, while he was a hero in his time, he has become an even larger figure in the annals of history. His courage and fighting spirit, as well as his value of duty and honor, are seen as the epitome of military leadership even to this day.

Though he was unable to defeat Xerxes and the Persians, he laid the groundwork that would lead to their eventual defeat and instilled a sense of confidence and duty in the Greek military forces. He and his men took a huge toll on the Persian army, in terms of number of casualties as well as demoralization of troops. His bravery and heroics would go on to inspire far more than just his fellow Greeks. Military leaders throughout history have looked upon Leonidas as an inspiration and a personal hero, from leaders in the United States and even in Nazi Germany during WWII.

Interestingly, the military leader that oversaw the ultimate defeat of the Persians has far less name recognition than Leonidas. It was his bravery in the face of insurmountable odds that continues to draw people to his legend and story.

Since his death, many statues, epic poems, and later, even comic books and movies, would be made about Leonidas and his legendary stand at Thermopylae. It should be stated that, while he was a legend in his time, his heroic legacy has had more of a long-term effect than it did an immediate one. We have to remember that at the time of his death, the Greeks were still at war and a year away from victory over the Persian forces.

8.

Leonidas laid the groundwork that would lead to their eventual defeat and instilled a sense of confidence and duty in the Greek military forces.

IMMEDIATE LEGACY

A monument dedicated to Leonidas and another for the 300 men who died with him in the final stand at Thermopylae was erected shortly after his death. His body was eventually returned to Sparta where he could be laid to rest in appropriate kingly and military fashion. His efforts, though unsuccessful, showed that wits and courage could stand in the face of brute strength and numbers.

While the battle at Thermopylae was lost, he and his small band of forces were able to hold off a huge number of Persian forces, leading to a mass of Persian casualties, due to strategy, better weaponry, and better military strategy. Though he lost and perished in his efforts, Leonidas' last stand at Thermopylae ignited pride in the Greek spirit and gave them the hope that they would eventually be successful against the Persians, and they were.

There were more failures that the Greeks had to endure before ultimate victory, but the Greeks refused to give up. Boeotia and Attica fell to the Persians; Athens was burned to the ground, and still, the Greeks would not surrender. After these defeats, the Greeks would win a stunning naval battle against Xerxes forces in Salamis, which led him to retreat, leaving behind a trusted military commander to continue with the battle.

Mardonius, the commander who Xerxes left in charge of the war, was soon to be outflanked. The Greeks amassed a huge hoplite force to take him on. The Battle of Plataea led to a massacre and defeat of Persian forces and the death of Mardonius. Simultaneously, the Greek navy destroyed what remained of the Persian navy in the Battle of Mycale. This stunning string of victories turned the proverbial tides of the war in the Greeks favor.

The Greeks were now on the offensive, not the defensive. They would continue to push back the Persians until they were finally defeated, and the second Greco-Persian war came to an end in 479 BC. The Greeks had, as the Oracle prophesied, prevailed over their enemies, and since the prophecy had been fulfilled, Greece was safe and the sovereignty of the nation maintained.

9.

*A monument dedicated to Leonidas and
another for the 300 men who died with him in
the final stand at Thermopylae was erected
shortly after his death.*

LEGENDARY LEGACY

Though Leonidas attained legendary status in his own times, it does seem that he has shone brighter in our modern times than he did in his own. This is likely due to the fact that at the time of his death, the Greeks were still engaged in battle and it was another military commander that oversaw the final victory. For the Greeks at the time, Leonidas was most certainly a figure worthy of honor and remembrance, but there also needed to be appropriate credit given to the military leaders who ultimately prevailed against Xerxes and the Persians.

The 20th and 21st centuries saw a dramatic resurgence in interest of Leonidas, as well as a huge groundswell of homage to his heroic self-sacrificing efforts. During this time, countless statues were dedicated to his honor. Epic poems would be written about his life and times. Famous movie stars would vie to play their part in films that detailed his fatal battle at Thermopylae. He was also to become the fascination of many military leaders throughout history. His ability to rally his forces, his cunning military strategy, and his courage and bravery would become a proverbial template that many military leaders wished to mold themselves after.

The "against all odds" story of the Battle of Thermopylae, as well as he and his troops willingness to lay down their lives for their country is a story that continues to resonate. Leonidas is often seen as the epitome of what it means to be a courageous and skillful soldier and leader, even in modern times. It was a short-lived event that was full of trial and tribulation, bravery and courage, and, of course, ultimate sacrifice, which will always make for a highly interesting story.

It has been said that many modern military leaders look up to Leonidas for his cunning and bravery. This, sadly, also included military personnel in Nazi Germany who propped up the willingness to sacrifice one's self as something that also defined German military character. This example was incredibly powerful during the devastating and unsuccessful attempts Germany made to invade Russia early on.

CONCLUSION

Though he ultimately died in his efforts, Leonidas is one of the best known and respected of all Grecian military leaders. He showed intense bravery and cunning, even in the face of insurmountable odds. He inspired in his own men, and in the minds of many military leaders that would come after, that self-sacrifice for the greater good is a laudable trait. It would be his willingness to sacrifice his life, and the sheer number of causalities his small band of forces were able to rack up that would give the Greeks the faith and confidence they needed to finally expel the Persians, though Leonidas would not be around to see this turn of events.

Leonidas was not born to be king; it was unfortunate life circumstance that would lead to his ascension to power. He had brothers ahead of him in line for the throne and, like most other Spartan boys, was sent for military training at the Agoge. Unfortunately, both his siblings died, leaving him the rightful heir to the throne. This was one of the first times in Spartan history that a king was also a trained military leader. However, it would end up being one of his greatest strengths as warfare was to be a significant part of his leadership duties

His training and upbringing made him uniquely suited to the times he served in. Shortly after taking the throne, word came to Greece that the Persians were planning an invasion. Leonidas went to seek the counsel of the famous Oracle at Delphi where he was told that a king must die in battle to ensure that continuation of Greece as a sovereign nation. He took this prophecy serious and interpreted it to mean that it must be him to die in battle. He accepted this fate bravely.

His most famous battle was the one in which he perished, the Battle of Thermopylae. Leading an outnumbered group of forces to try to hold the mountain pass that the Persians had to cross to enter the Grecian mainland, he was able to fend off the massive Persian force for some three days. The Greeks were ultimately betrayed by one of their own who told the Persians of a circuitous route that would lead them into the mainland and allow them to bypass the bulk of the Greek forces.

Once he knew what was happening, Leonidas made the fateful decision to send most of his troops away. He and a group of some 300 hoplites were all that remained to stop the Persian invasion. He ordered his men to fight to the death and in a heroic last stand, Leonidas and his group of men were able to take down a huge number of Persians before they would all perish in battle.

Though his efforts were unsuccessful, his bravery and courage in the face of all odds was an inspiration to the Greeks which would end up propelling them to victory against the Persians in

CONCLUSION

the end. He would go on to become a legendary war hero that we continue to study to this day.

THE LEGACY OF LEONIDAS I

A NOTE FROM T.D. VAN BASTEN

Thank you very much for reading The Legacy of Leonidas I. If you enjoyed it and found what you were looking for, please be so kind to take a moment to leave a review at your favourite retailer such as Amazon.

–T.D. van Basten

THE LEGACY OF LEONIDAS I

ABOUT THE AUTHOR

Losing sense of time through television and technology, many seem to have forgotten about our ancestors and how the world has been shaped to what it is today. T.D. van Basten has set the tone for historical coverage and is admired by many for his exceptional passion, vivid descriptions and storytelling.

THE LEGACY OF LEONIDAS I

ANCIENT GREECE BIOGRAPHIES

THE LEGACY OF ALEXANDER THE GREAT

Alexander III of Macedon, better known to the world as Alexander the Great, was one of the most powerful rulers of the ancient world. During his time, he amassed the largest amount of land that the Greek empire would ever see. He seemed to capture land with ease and managed to spread the culture and language of the Greek empire far and wide, ushering in what is referred to as the Hellenic Period.

It was during the time of his father that the various Greek city-states came together under a single ruler. Dubbed the League of Corinth, it was comprised of all the regional city-states and Philip II was the sole leader of the League. He was, unfortunately, unexpectedly assassinated at his daughter's wedding, which threw the League and Macedonia into a bit of chaos.

THE LEGACY OF ARISTOTLE

We have all heard of Aristotle. A pillar of the classical world of ancient Greece, he was one of the first and greatest philosophers to ever exist. Without him, our world and the Western intellectual tradition would be simply unrecognizable. Aristotle studied, and wrote and lectured on, every academic discipline you could probably ever imagine. His existence and work were critically important parts of the foundation of every subject of philosophy and science in existence today.

In this book, we will explore the dynamic, fascinating life of this great thinker. We will begin with his birth and boyhood, and then move on to his twenty years studying and teaching at the legendary Platonic Academy in Athens, his time in Assos (which included marriage and leading a group of philosophers of his own), his life at the Macedonian court acting as private tutor to a young Alexander the Great, and finally the years he spent running his own school, The Lyceum, in Athens. We will also discuss the philosopher's works, as well as his general contribution to, and immense influence on, the Western intellectual tradition.

THE LEGACY OF SOCRATES

The philosophy of Socrates glitters until today and will continue doing so in the future. Socrates is not the actual founder of philosophy, as is sometimes claimed. Preceding him, and as the name suggests, there were the pre-Socratic philosophers. Some of them are Pythagoras, Thales, Empedocles, Parmenides and Heraclitus of Ephesus. However, Socrates is the founder of the logos (discourse). For example, a rational, coherent thought, which gradually releases the myth. He distrusted writing and teaching and was therefore exclusively oral. Everything we know about him comes from the testimony of others, and most importantly, his student, Plato.

Socrates was born in Athens, 470 BC. He was the son of a sculptor named Sophroniscus, and a midwife named Phaenarete. He was also a sculptor himself, but he devoted his life entirely to philosophy. He was first pointed out by the originality of his speeches and his way of life. He was barefoot, resisted thirst and hunger, bore the cold, helped men and young people in the street, questioned them and motivated them. He was a sort of apostle who dreamed of bringing his people to virtue and to reorganize his city, making it bigger, stronger and more radiant. He was also a mystic man.

THE LEGACY OF ACHILLES

The legend of Achilles is one of the greatest legends in the Greek mythology and one of its oldest. His fame survived through centuries and his legend is enhanced by thousands of details in the Iliad poem. Achilles' best traits are glory and honor, he was so eager to follow these exploits with his inseparable friend Patroclus. He preferred, despite the multiple warnings of his mother Thetis, a short but glorious life. Thetis' beauty, bravery, fortitude and valuable protection that she provided to Achilles would grant him the approval of Greek Goddesses, such as Hera and Athena, which greatly helped him to increase his fame.

He was actually more than just a hero; Achilles was considered in ancient times as a demi-god and revered in many parts of Greece. He dedicated his entire life to pursuing a glorious afterlife, seeking to be surrounded by his deities with whom he shared his life and pleasures in an eternal joy atmosphere, interspersed with feasting and fighting endlessly for the sake of honor and greatness.